ECONOMICS

WORKBOOK

DR. MOHIT KUMAR JINDAL

To my wife...

Contents

Preface

Welcome to "Economics workbook: A Comprehensive Workbook for Understanding Economic Principles and Applications." This workbook is designed to provide students with a comprehensive understanding of the fundamental principles of economics and how they can work on it in the classroom.

This workbook seeks to demystify economics by presenting the material in a clear and accessible way, . Whether you are a student, a business professional, or simply interested in learning more about economics through class room or online , this workbook is an essential resource that will help you navigate the complexities of the Economics.

Chapter by chapter, book covers the essential principles of economics, starting with the basic concepts of supply and demand and moving on to more complex topics such as cost, production National income and its aggreats .

In each chapter, Students will find a left page blank for exercises and review questions and prepareing the daigrams that help to reinforce the material covered in the chapter. We hope you find this workbook informative, engaging, and useful, and we look forward to hearing your feedback as you work through the material.

Acknowledgements

We would like to express our sincere thanks and gratitude to everyone who contributed to the creation of "Economics workbook: A Comprehensive Workbook for Understanding Economic Principles and Applications." This workbook would not have been possible without the dedication and support of a wide range of individuals and organizations.

First and foremost, we would like to thank our colleagues and peers in the field of economics for their invaluable insights and feedback. Their expertise and knowledge have been instrumental in shaping the content of this workbook and ensuring that it accurately reflects the latest developments in the field.

We would also like to extend our thanks to the students and educators who have used earlier versions of this workbook and provided valuable feedback and suggestions for improvement. Their feedback has been essential in refining the material and making it more engaging and accessible to a wider audience.

We are grateful to the editorial team at the publishing company for their guidance and support throughout the publishing process. Their professionalism and expertise have been essential in ensuring that the final product is of the highest quality and meets the needs of the target audience.

We would like to thank our families and friends for their love, support, and encouragement throughout the development of this workbook. Their unwavering support has been a source of inspiration and motivation, and we are grateful for their patience and understanding during this process.

Finally, we would like to express our gratitude to the readers of this workbook, whether you are a student, a business professional, or simply interested in learning more about economics. We hope that this workbook provides you with a clear and comprehensive understanding of the fundamental principles of economics and their applications, and that it helps you navigate the complexities of the modern economy.

Thank you all for your contributions and support. We hope that this workbook serves as a valuable resource and reference for years to come.

CHAPTER ONE

CONCEPTS OF ECONOMICS

Meaning of Economics:

The study of those activities of human beings which are concerned with the satisfaction of unlimited wants by utilizing limited resources is known as economics.

Economics is the study of how economic agents or societies *choose* to use *scarce* productive resources that have *alternative uses* to satisfy wants which are *unlimited* and of *varying degrees of importance.*

The main concern of economics is economic problem: its identification, description, explanation and solution, if possible. The source of any economic problem is scarcity.

Scarcity of resources forces economic agents to choose among alternatives. Therefore, economic problem can be said to be a problem of choice and valuation of alternatives. The problem of choice arises because limited resources with alternative uses are to be utilized to satisfy unlimited wants, which are of varying degrees of importance. Had the resources like human, natural, capital, etc. not been scarce, there would have been no problem of choice and hence no economic problem at all. Therefore, the root cause of all economic problems is scarcity.

Definition of Economics: It has been broadly divided into four parts.

a. Adam smith's wealth. Definition.
b. Marshall's welfare definition.
c. Lionel Robin's scarcity definition.

d. Samuelson's growth oriented definition.

1. *Wealth definition:* According to Adam Smith' economics is concerned with " an inquiry into the nature and causes of wealth of nations" and it related to the laws of production, exchange, distribution and consumption of wealth.

2. *Welfare definition:* According to Dr. Marshall, "Economics is a study of mankind in the ordinary business of life, it examinees that part of individual and social action which is most closely connected with the attainment and with the use of material requisites of well being thus, it is on one side a study of wealth, on the other and more important side a part of the study of man"

3. *Scarcity definition:* According to Lionel Robbins "Economics is a science which studies human behaviour as a relationship between ends and scarce means which have alternative uses."

4. *Growth- oriented definition:* According to Prof. Samuelson, " Economics is the study of how people and society end up choosing with or without the use of money, to employ scarce productive resources that could have alternative uses top produce various commodities over time and distributing them for consumption, now or in the future, among various persons and groups in society. It analyses costs and benefits of improving patterns of resource allocation "

Different Economic Systems:

Every economy faces three fundamental questions in its functioning. These are –

a. What goods and services are to produce and in what quantity?
b. How to produce those goods and services? I.e. how the scarce resources are optimally allocated? And
c. How the goods and services so produced are distributed among the households?

The nature of an economic system depends on how the above questions are resolved and who co-ordinates the decisions of millions of economic agents.

• 4 •

Based on the above, there are three types of economic systems viz.

1. Capitalist economic system: " Capitalist economy may be defined as that system of economic organization in which free enterprise, competition and the private ownership of property generally prevail." - R.T.Bye.

Features:

1. Private Property.
2. Price Mechanism.
3. Freedom of Enterprise.
4. Sovereignty of the consumer.
5. Competition and Co-operation.
6. Profit Motive
7. No government interference.
8. Democratic.
9. Less Burden on government.
10. Self-interest

2. Socialist economic system: " Socialism refers to the government ownership of the means of production, planning by the government and income redistribution " - Samuelson,

Features:

1. Collective ownership
2. Economic, Social and Political Equality.
3. Set objectives.
4. Positive Role of government.
5. Work according to ability and wage according to need.
6. Economic Planning.
7. Lack of competition.

8. Maximum Social Welfare.

3. *Mixed economy:* "Mixed economy is that economy in which both public and private sector co-operate, is called as mixed economy" - Samuelson.

Features:

1. Co- existence of Public and Private Sector.
2. Individual freedom.
3. Economic Planning.
4. Private Property is allowed.
5. Economic Equality.
6. Price Mechanism and
7. Profit motive and social welfare.
8. Role of the government.

SCOPE OF ECONOMICS

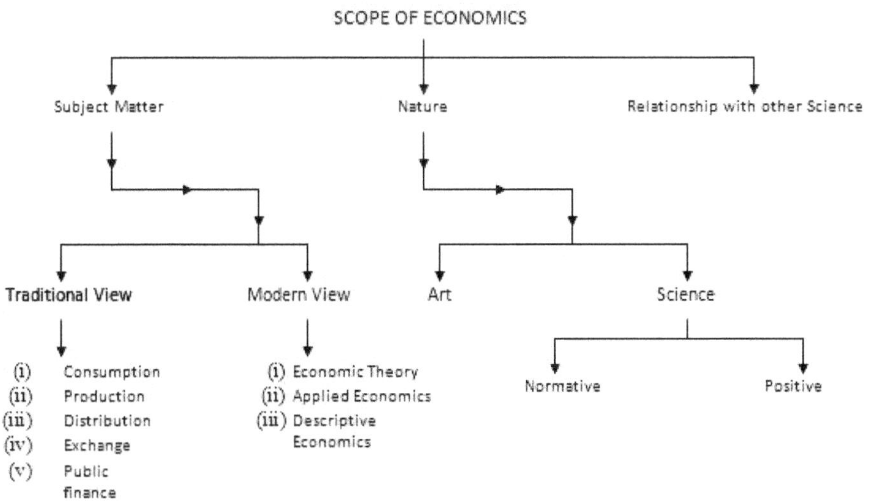

Scope of Economics

•8•

Classification of economics

Positive and Normative Economics: Positive economics is a study or analysis of facts. It indicates 'how things are'. Normative economics, by contrast, studies on 'what ought to be'. By another way, normative economics is considered with the judgmental aspects, while positive economics is considered with actual facts.

Micro economics: Microeconomics is concerned with the behavior of individual entities like markets, firms, and households.

Importance:

i. Operation of an Economy.
ii. Economic Policies.
iii. Predictions.
iv. Economic Welfare.
v. Solving specific Problems

Limitations:

i. Unrealistic Assumptions,
ii. Static Analysis.
iii. Wrong conclusions.
iv. Abstract Nature

Macro Economics: Macroeconomics is study of economy as a whole. Macroeconomics is concerned with changes in total output, total employment, CPI, exports and imports.

Importance:

i. Working of the Economy.
ii. Formulation of Economic Policies.
iii. Solution of Economic Problems.
iv. Changes in Price level.
v. Study of trade cycle.
vi. Helpful in Economic Planning.

Limitations:

i.   Ignorance of individual altogether.
ii. Individual differences overlooked.

Economic Models:

" A model is an organised set of relationship that describes. The functions of an economic entity, whether it be a household, a single industry or a national economy under a set of simplified assumptions"

TYPES:

A. *Aggregate Model:* This model is applicable to the whole economy and treat production, consumption and investment as a single aggregate.
B. *Sector Model:* This model is formulated for individual sectors like agriculture, industry, banking, trade, telecommunication, etc,
C. *Inter - industry Model:* This model is concerned with the relationship of the different producing sectors of an economy.

Adam Smith

CHAPTER TWO

DEMAND ANALYSIS

<u>Meaning of Demand</u>:

Demand for a good refers to the quantity of the good that a consumer wants to, is willing to and is able to buy at a price, during a specified period of time.
Demand = Want + Willingness + Ability

Demand Function:

As mentioned above that an individual household's demand for a commodity depends on the household's desire for the commodity and its capability. The desire to purchase is revealed by tastes and preference of the households. The capability to purchase depends upon his purchasing power, which is depends upon income and price of the commodity. The quantity of a particular commodity depends upon price of that and price of other commodities.

So, demand of X commodity depends

1. Price Of The Commodity (Px)
2. Prices Of Substitutes (Ps) And Complements (Pc)
3. Income Of The Household (Y)
4. Tastes And Preference Of The Households (T), And
5. Expectation Of Future Price Change (Ep)

$Dx = f (Px, Ps, Pc, Y, T, \ldots\ldots Ep)$

.

.

.

Detail of determinates:

(1) <u>Price of the commodity:</u> generally, a household is willing to purchase more of commodity when its price is low and vice versa. Thus there is negative relationship between quantity demanded and price.

(2) <u>Price of related commodities:</u> when a change in the price of the other commodity leaves the amount demanded of commodity unchanged it is called independent commodity or unrelated. Related commodities are two types;

a. *Substitutes commodity*: when the price of one commodity and the quantity demanded of the other commodity have positive relation. (Fig 1)
b. *Complements commodity*: when the price of one commodity and the quantity demanded of the other commodity have negative relation.(Fig 2)

(3) <u>Income of the household:</u> with an increase in income, a household increases the consumption of the normal commodities. But in the case of certain commodity like foods, fruits, vegetables, etc., demand increases at a certain level with the increase in income.

(4) <u>Tastes and preference of the households:</u> the favorable change in tastes and preference of the household, results greater demand and vice versa.

Demand Curve and Schedule:

Demand schedule shows how the quantity demanded of a good varies with price, other things being constant in a tabular form. The graphical representation of demand schedule is called demand curve.

Law of Demand:

This is also known as the first law of purchase. It indicates the relation between the price of a commodity its quantity demanded in the market. The law may be stated as,

Law of demand states that "all other things remaining constant, as price falls, the quantity demanded rises and vice versa". This negative relationship between price and quantity demanded is apparent by the shape of the demand curve.

Assumption of law: we assume,

1. That people's incomes remain unchanged,
2. That the prices of other related commodity remain unchanged,
3. That the tastes of the consumer remain unchanged
4. That the people do not have expectation further change in the price of the commodity, and
5. That the commodity in question is not one which has a 'prestige value', such as, diamonds etc.

Why does the law of demand operate?

According to Hicks, "there is an inverse relationship between the price and quantity demanded, when price increases quantity demanded falls down."

There are four reasons for the operation of the law:

1. Law of Diminishing marginal utility
2. Principal of different user
3. Income effect
4. Substitution effect.

Exception of the law of demand:

1. The Giffen paradox: a fall in its price tends to reduce and a rise in its price tends to extend its demand.
2. Snob effect: refers to the desire to own exclusive or unique goods
3. Expectations: When a consumer expects the price of a good to increase in future, he may buy more of that good to reduce loss.
4. Veblen effect: Some consumers judge the quality of a good by its price. This type of consumer behavior is known as Veblen effect.

Types of demand:

1. *Autonomous demand*: when the demand of a commodity directly satisfies some wants.
2. *Derived demand*: when the demand for a commodity depends upon the demand for its final product.
3. *Composite demand*: when a commodity put to several uses.
4. *Joint demand*: when several things are needed to make a commodity.
5. *Cross demand*: it refers to the different quantity of a commodity which will be brought as a result of change in the price of related goods.

Movement along a demand curve and shift in a demand curve

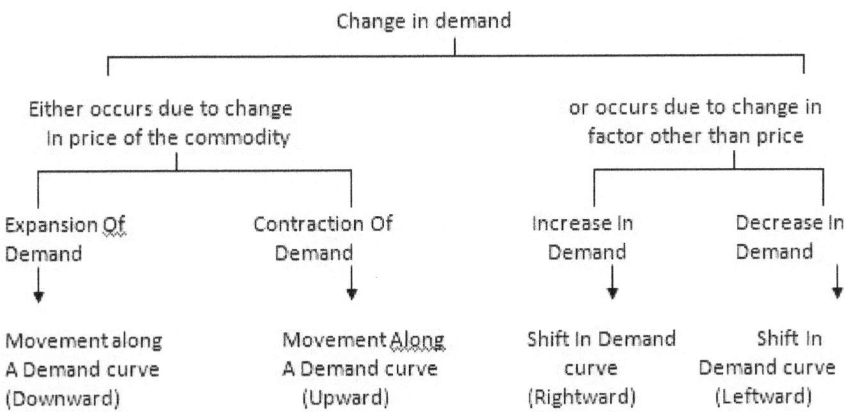

Movement along a demand curve and shift in a demand curve

Elasticity of demand:

Demand elasticity is simply a measure of relative responsiveness of quantity demanded to change in one of determinates, other determinates assumed as unchanged. To a specific, elasticity of demand (e d) is defined as the ratio of the percentage change in quantity demanded to the percentage change in the demand determinant under consideration. That is,

$$E\,d = \frac{\text{Percentage change in quantity demanded of good X}}{\text{Percentage change in determinant Z}}$$

Elasticity of Demand

Z determinates may be:

1. Current price of the commodity
2. Current price of related goods
3. Current income

Price Elasticity of demand:

The measure of relative responsiveness of quantity demanded to price along a given demand curve is known as price elasticity of demand.

$$Edp = \frac{\text{Percentage change in quantity demanded of good X}}{\text{Percentage change in price of good X}}$$

Price Elasticity of Demand

Types:

- Perfectly elastic demand (e =)

- Absolutely inelastic demand (e = 0)
- Unit elasticity demand (e = 1)
- Relatively elastic demand (e >1)
- Relatively inelastic demand (e <1)

Point and Arc price elasticity of demand

The elasticity computed at a single point on the demand curve for an infinitesimal change in the price is called point elasticity. The elasticity computed between two separate points on the demand curve is called arc' elasticity.

<u>Point elasticity</u>

The Point elasticity of demand is defined as the proportionate change in quantity demanded resulting from a very small change in price of that commodity.

Point e p =

<u>Arc elasticity</u>

Arc elasticity is a measure of the average responsiveness to the price change over a finite stretch on the demand curve.

Arc e p =

Measurement of price elasticity of demand

<u>Percentage method</u>:

in this case, elasticity of demand is measured as percent (proportionate) change in quantity demanded divided by percent (proportionate) change in price of that commodity.

<u>Slope method</u>:

.

elasticity of demand can be measured with the help of a tangent. A tangent is drawn at the point on the demand curve whose elasticity is to be found. The elasticity of demand at that point is simply the ratio of the two portions of the tangent,

Point e p = lower segment of the demand curve/Upper segment of the demand curve

Mathematical method:

the point elasticity can also be calculated mathematically in which case we need to use the concept of differential calculus.

Point e p =

Outlay method:

another method of measuring elasticity of demand is through observing "how the price change affects the total revenue of the firm through influencing the quantity demanded of that commodity."

	Elasticity less Than unitary $(e < 1)$	Unit elastic $(e = 1)$	elasticity greater than unitary $(e > 1)$
Price Rise	Total Revenue RISES	Total Revenue UNCHAHGED	Total Revenue FALLS
Price fall	Total Revenue FALLS	Total Revenue UNCHAHGED	Total Revenue RISES

Outlay Method

Determinants of price elasticity of demand:

1. <u>The Number and Closeness of the Substitutes</u>: in case the product has a large number of close substitutes in the price range under consideration, demand for the product bound to be highly elastic.

1. <u>The Share of the Commodity in Buyer's Budget</u>: if the proportion of consumer's income which is spent on the commodity is very small, demand will tend to be inelastic.
2. <u>Nature of the Commodity:</u> it is generally believed that the demand for necessities is inelastic, while those of luxuries elastic.

4. <u>Number of Uses a Commodity can be put to</u>: larger the number of uses of a commodity greater will be the elasticity of that commodity.

5. <u>Habit-Forming Characteristic</u>: If the consumer forms a habit for their use, the demand for such product will tend to be inelastic.

6. <u>Time Period</u>: demand is more elastic in the long run that in the short run because we know longer the time period considered, greater will be the possibility of substituting the commodity under consideration will be cheaper commodity.

Income elasticity of demand

Income elasticity of demand for a commodity shows the extent to which a consumer's demand for a commodity change as a result of change in his income.

$$E_y$$
=Percentage change in quantity demanded of good X/Percentage change in the consumer's income

$E_y =$

<u>Types:</u>

1. Highly income elastic
2. Unitary income elastic
3. Low income elastic
4. Zero income elastic
5. Negative income elastic

.

.

.

• 28 •

Cross elasticity of demand

Cross elasticity of demand is defined as the ratio of the percentage change in the demand for one goods to the percentage change in the price of some other good.

e x y =

For the perfectly substitute products the cross elasticity of demand is highly positive and generally tends to infinity. And, for the perfectly complementary goods the cross elasticity of the demand will be highly negative, tending to infinity (negative).

Importance of elasticity of demand:

1. <u>Level of output and price</u>: if production is to be profitable, the volume of goods and services produced must be in accordance with the demand for the commodity. And note that demand change with the change in the price. In a competitive market the elasticity of demand for a commodity is inelastic, he can charge the high price for it.
2. <u>Fixation of reward for factor of production</u>: for example if the demand for the workers is inelastic efforts of trade union to rise wages of the worker will meet with success, otherwise not.
3. <u>Government policies:</u>

(a) when fixing the rate of exchange for its currency the government can take considerable help from the concept of the elasticity of demand, when taking decision to revalue or devalue the currency the government has to carefully study the impact of such a decision.

(b) Ed is also help to government in its taxation policy. It is with the help of elasticity of demand and supply that the government can find out as to how much burden of addition taxation will be borne by whom.

4. <u>Demand forecasting</u>: while price and cross elasticities are useful for pricing policy, income elasticity can be used for forecasting demand for the product in future.

We, Thus, find that the concept of elasticity of demand is very important in different feces of economic decision- making.

CHAPTER THREE

SUPPLY ANALYSIS

Meaning of supply:

Supply of a commodity refers to the various quantities of commodity which a seller willing and able to sell at different prices in a given market, at a point of time, other things remaining the same. Supply is related to scarcity, it is only the scarce goods which have a supply price; the goods which are freely available have no supply price.

Supply function:

The amount of a commodity supplied depends upon a number of factors. These can be stated in the terms of a supply function:

S x = f (P x, P y, P f,........ O, T)

P x = price of the good x

P y = price of other goods in the market

P f = prices of factor of production needed to produce good x

O = objective of the producer

T = state of technology used by the producer to produce good x

Determinates:

- <u>Price of the goods which is to be supplied:</u> the amount of supply increases when produces get a higher price for their product, other thing being equal.
- <u>Prices of other goods:</u> prices of different commodities move in the different directions. These have influence on the supply of a commodity.

- <u>Price of factors of production:</u> a rise in the factor prices will result in reduction in the amount supplied.
- <u>Producer's objectives</u>: producers differ in terms of their objectives- some may be interested in maximizing profits, while other in maximizing sales revenue or creating goodwill, etc.
- <u>State of technology</u>: a change in technology brought about by an invention may lower costs of production and would enable to supply increased quantity at a given price.

Supply schedule:

A tabular statement of price-quantity relationship is known as the supply schedule.

Supply curve:

A supply curve is a graphical presentation of a supply schedule. When price-quantity information of supply is plotted on a graph, a supply curve is drawn.

Law of supply:

The quantity supplied depends upon a number of factors. If we start considering the influence of all these factors simultaneously on the amount supplied of a commodity, we will not be able to develop any simple law of supply. Law of supply state that 'other things remaining constant more of a commodity is supplied at a higher price and less of it supplied at lower price.

Assumptions of the law:

1. There is no change in the prices of the factors of production.
2. There is no change in the technique of production.
3. There is no change in the goal of the firm.
4. There is no change in the price of related goods.

Exception of law

1. Agricultural products whose supplies are governed by natural factors.
2. Social distinction

Movement along a supply curve and shift in a supply curve

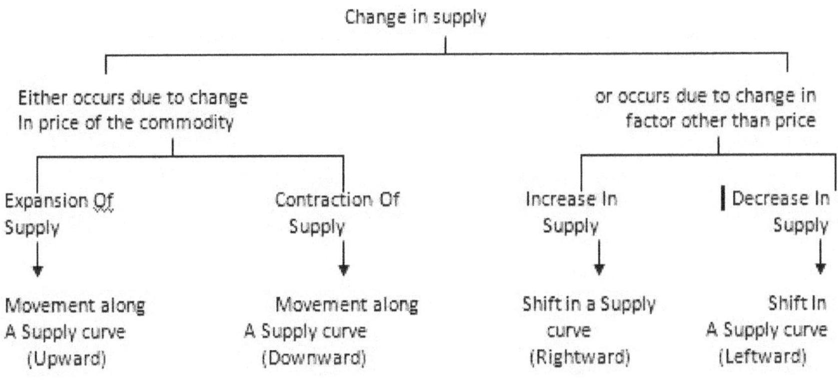

Movement along a supply curve and shift in a supply curve

<u>Elasticity of supply:</u>

It is defined as the responsiveness of the sellers to a change in the price of the commodity. It point out the reactions of the sellers to a particular change in the price of the commodity. Elasticity determines the steepness of the slope of the supply curve. The steeper the slope, the more inelastic is the supply.

e s = Percentage change in quantity supplied/ Percentage change in price

Types:

1. Perfectly elastic supply (e =)
2. Absolutely inelastic supply (e = 0)
3. Unit elasticity supply (e = 1)
4. Relatively elastic supply (e >1)
5. Relatively inelastic supply (e <1)

Measurement of elasticity of supply

Percentage method:

in this case, elasticity of supply is measured as percent (proportionate) change in quantity supplied divided by percent (proportionate) change in price of that commodity.

e s =

Geometric method: geometrically elasticity of supply is depends upon the 'origin' of the supply curve.

Es = 1, when an upward sloping, straight line supply curve starts from the origin

Es > 1, when an upward sloping, straight line supply curve starts from the Y- axis.

Es < 1, when an upward sloping, straight line supply curve starts from the X- axis.

Zero elasticity of supply

Infinity elasticity of supply

Factor influencing elasticity of supply

1. <u>Time:</u> the longer the period of time, the more elastic is the supply likely to be.

1. <u>Nature of the industry</u>: in the case of heavy industry supply of its bound to be inelastic, the

reason being that such an industry requires specialized equipment and machinery not able to quick increases in the short period. In the case of light one, requiring only ordinary appliances, its output can be increased quickly even during the short period.

3. <u>ost of production</u>: under the law of diminishing production then the supply of such a commodity will be inelastic.

4. <u>Nature of the product</u>: if the commodity is non-durable, elasticity of supply will be inelastic, on the hand in the case of durable elasticity of supply will be elastic because its supply can be increased on the rise of its price.

5. <u>Price level</u>: higher the price level higher greater the supply.

6. <u>High/lower taxation.</u>

7. <u>Number of sellers</u>

Alfred Marshall

• 40 •

CHAPTER FOUR

COST ANALYSIS

Concept of Cost

Money cost:

The most widely accepted concept of cost is the money cost of production. It means the aggregate money expenditure incurred by a firm on the various items entering into the production of a commodity.

Explicit costs or Paid-out costs or Expenditure costs

+ Implicit costs i.e., cost of these resources and services which are used by the producer but the payment is not made directly by him or producer's own resources and services offered to the business

+ Normal profit, i.e., that level of profit which is just sufficient to induce him to stay in the business.

Real cost:

The exertions of all the different kinds of labour that are directly or indirectly involved in making it, together with the abstinences or rather the waiting required for saving the capital used in making it; all these efforts and sacrifices together will be called the real cost of that commodity.

Opportunity costs:

Opportunity cost is concerned with the cost of forgone opportunities. In other words, it is the comparison between the policy that was chosen and policy that was rejected. The concept of opportunity cost focuses attention

on the net revenue that could be generated in the next best use of a scarce input.

Actual cost:

Actual costs are the costs which the firm incurs while producing or acquiring a good or a service like the cost on raw material, labour, rent, interest, etc.

Accounting costs:

Accounting costs are the actual or outlay costs. These costs point out how much expenditure has already been incurred on a particular process or on production as such.

Economic costs:

Economic costs related to future. They are in the nature of the incremental costs the imputed and the explicit costs as well as the opportunity costs.

Replacement and original or historical costs:

Historical cost of an asset states the cost of plant, equipment and materials at the price paid originally for them, while the replacement costs state the cost the firm would have to incur if it want to replace or acquire the same assts now.

Direct cost:

Direct costs are that are readily identified and are traceable to a particular product, operation or plant. Evan overhead can be direct as to a department; the manufacturing costs can be direct to a product line, sales territory, etc.

Indirect costs:

These cost are not readily identified nor visibly traceable to specific goods, services, operations, etc. but are nevertheless charged to the jobs or products in standard accounting practice.

• 44 •

Incremental costs:

The difference in the cost as a result of a change in the level or the nature of business activity is called incremental cost or differential cost.

Sunk cost:

Sunk costs are costs that are not altered by a change in quantity and cannot be recovered.

Cost function

A cost function is the mathematical relationship between the cost of a product and the various determinants of cost.

Symbolically,

$C = f (S, O, P, T...)$

C = cost

S = size of firm

O = level of output

P = price of inputs

T = technology

Costs in the short run:

Total cost: "Total cost" represents the lowest total rupees expense needed to produce each level of output q. TC rises as q rises.

Fixed cost: "Fixed cost" represents the total rupees expense that goes on even when a zero output is produced. It is sunk cost that is completely unaffected by any variation in q.

Variable cost: "Variable cost" represents all items of TC except for FC- including raw materials, wages, fuel, etc. which change with the level of firm's output.

By definition,

TC = FC + VC

Marginal cost: marginal cost at any output level q is the extra cost of production of producing 1 extra unit more (or less); it comes from subtracting total cost rupees costs of adjacent outputs.

$$MC = TC_n - TC_{n-1}$$

.

Quantity	Fixed cost	Variable cost	Total cost	Marginal cost
0	55	0		
1		30		
2		55		
3		75		
4		105		
5		155		
6		225		

Calculation of Cost

Average fixed cost (AFC): average fixed cost is the total fixed cost divided by the number of units produced. Thus,

AFC =

Average variable cost (AVC): average variable cost is the total variable cost divided by the number of unit produced. Thus,

AVC =

Average cost (AC): average cost is the total cost divided by the number of unit produced. Since the total cost is the sum of total variable cost and total fixed cost, average cost is also the sum of average variable cost and average fixed cost.

AC = AFC + AVC

AC =

.

.

.

Quantity q	Fixed cost FC	Variable cost VC	Total cost TC= FC+VC	Marginal cost MC	Average cost AC= TC/q	Average variable cost AVC= VC/q	Average fixed cost AFC= FC/q
0	55	0					
1		30					
2		55					
3		75					
4		105					
5		155					
6		225					
7		315					
8		425					
9		555					
10		705					

Calculation of Cost

Curves - AC, AVC, AFC, MC

Note: MC intersects the U-shaped AC at AC's minimum. This is no coincidence. To left of intersect point, MC < AC and hence is pulling AC down. To the right, MC>AC and hence is pulling AC up. At the point AC=MC; hence AC is horizontal there, being neither raised nor lowered by the equivalent MC. Also, MC cuts the AVC curve exactly at is bottom.

At the bottom of U-shaped AC, **MC=AC= minimum AC.**

.

.

CHAPTER FIVE

PRODUCTION ANALYSIS

Production

Production is an activity that create utility or value. It includes any process that transforms input output, thus adding to the utility which the consumer could have derived form inputs. Production theory is applicable not only to the production, distribution and storage of tangible goods; it can also be applied to service activities. In fact, production is any activity that increases consumer usability of goods and services.

<u>Usability can be added:</u>

1. By changing the form
2. By changing the place
3. By supplying goods at an appropriate time

Factor of production

The term factor of production refers to those goods and services which aid the productive process. Production is not possible without the co-operation of factor of production; generally four factors of production are recognized. These are – land, labour, capital and entrepreneur.

Land

Land stands for all natural recourses such as forest, lakes, seas and mountains, minerals, etc which yield an income or which have exchange value. It resents those natural resources which are useful and scare,

actually or potentially.

<u>Characteristics of land</u>

1. Land is fixed in supply
2. Land is free gift of nature
3. Land cannot be destroyed
4. Land is immobile
5. Land differs in fertility and situation
6. Land is a passive (not active) factor of production

Important of land

1. Most important factor of production
2. Economic development
3. Development of primary industries
4. Development of manufacturing industries
5. Development of the means of transport and communication
6. Chief agent in the production of wage goods

Labour

Labour consists of all human efforts of body or mind, which are undertaken, in the expectation of reward.

1. It can be mental as well as physical
2. Undertaken in the expectation of a reward

<u>Characteristics</u>

1. Labour of perishable
2. Labour has weaker bargaining power
3. Labour is an active factor of production
4. Labour cannot be separated form the labourer
5. The labour sells his labour, but not himself
6. Labour is mobile

7. Supply of labour is inelastic

Factors determining efficiency of labour

1. Social environment

    a. Climate
    b. Social customs
    c. Religious effect

2. Factor atmosphere

    a. Working conditions
    b. Length of working hours
    c. Reward
    d. Freedom, hope for future progress and variety in work
    e. Social security and welfare schemes

3. Ability of management
4. Personal qualities of workers

    a. Standard of living
    b. Education

5. Other factors

    a. Mobility of labour
    b. Trade union movement

Capital

In economics, the term 'capital' refers to that part of man-made wealth which is used for the further production of wealth. Thus tools, machines of all kinds, buses, trucks, railways, factory premises, raw materials, etc., are all included in the category of capital because they help in the production of further goods.

<u>Characteristics</u>

1. Capital is a passive factor of production
2. Capital in man made
3. Capital has the highest mobility
4. Supply of capital is elastic
5. Capital is productive
6. Capital consume long time
7. Capital involves present sacrifice (cost) in return for future values (benefit)

Types of capital

<u>Physical capital and human capital</u>

All physical goods such as building, plant and machinery etc. are called physical capital. On the other hand human skill and ability come under human capital.

Individual capital and social capital

Property owned by an individual or group of individuals is called Individual capital. As against this, property owned by society as a whole, such as road, bridge etc. Is called social capital.

Fixed and circulating capital

Fixed capital is durable in nature and circulating capital has only one time use, like raw materials etc.

Tangible and intangible capital

Tangible capital can be perceived by senses (material capital) whereas intangible capital cannot be perceived by senses (patent right, trademark, skill, goodwill, etc)

Real and money or portfolio capital

Those assets which aid the productive process such as machinery, plant etc. the latter, however, points to shares, debentures, bonds and stock certificates in term of which money is generally invested in expectation of returns.

Capital formation

Capital formation means an addition to the stock of capital goods in the country. The capital goods comprise such things as machinery, plant, power, and etc. such capitals are used for further production of wealth.

Factor governing capital formation

1. Saving

    a. Saving by households

        i. Power to save
        ii. Willingness to save

    b. Savings by big business corporations (Corporation sector)
    c. Saving by the government (Government sector)

2. Mobilizing of saving
3. Investment

    Entrepreneur
    An entrepreneur is a person who combines the different factor of production (land, labour, capital), in the right proportion and initiates the process of production and also bears the risk involved in it.
    <u>Function of entrepreneur</u>

1. Organizing production

*   Choice of industry

• 60 •

- Choice of commodities and services
- Deciding the size of production
- Scale of production

1. Organizing production

    I. Choice of industry
    II. Choice of commodities and services
    III. Deciding the size of production
    IV. Scale of production
    V. Optimum factor combination of the factor of production
    VI. Location of the production unit

2. Risk taking and uncertainty bearing
3. Innovation

Qualities of an entrepreneur

1. Intelligence and ability of high order
2. Capacity to take quick decisions
3. Full and complete knowledge of his business
4. Capacity to recognize the worth and ability of a person
5. Quality of farsightedness
6. Inspire confidence in other
7. Knowledge about the latest development
8. Develop his capacity to face difficulties

Production function

Production function is the purely technical relationship which connects factor inputs and outputs. Production function includes all the technically efficient methods of production. Thus, production function specifies a flow of output resulting from a flow of input during a specified period time. Production function rest of two main assumptions:

- Technology is invariant.

- It is assumed that firms utilize their inputs at the maximum levels of efficiency.
- Factor of production are divisible into variable units.
- It is related to a specific period of time.

The production function in generally written in the form of an equation:
Q = f (L, N, K...)
Q = Output
L = land
N = labour
K = capital

In economic theory we are generally concerned with three types of production functions:

1. Production function with one variable factor-<u>Short Run Production Function</u>
2. Production function with all variable factor- <u>Long Run Production Function</u>
3. Production function with two variable factor- <u>Cobb-Douglas Production Function</u>

Production function with one variable factor

Short Run Production Function

The law states that with a given state of technology if a quantity of one factor input increased, by equal increment the quantities of the other factor remain fixed, the production firstly increases but decreases, after a particular point.

The law of diminishing retunes to factor (Law of Variable Proportion) state that as we go on employing more of one factor of production, other remain constant. Its marginal productivity will diminish after a particular point. It can be seen that if law holds then the total product curve will also behave in a similar manner, it will be initially be upward sloping and then after some point start sloping downwards.

Assumption of law:

1. The state of technology remain the constant
2. One factor of production always be kept constant at a give level
3. Law is not applicable when the two inputs are used in fixed proportion.

Table & Diagram

The three stages of the production
1st STAGE:

In the beginning the quantity of fixed factors are more relatively to the quantity of variable factor. Therefore when more or more units of variable factor added to the constant quantity of fixed factor then fixed factor more intensively and effectively utilized i.e. efficiency of fixed factor increases at addition unit of variable unit added to it, this causes production increase at a rapid.

When the variable factors are relatively less, some amount of fixed factor remains unutilized. When additional unit of variable factors increased, fully utilization of fixed factor become possible with the result increasing return to factor is obtained.

1st stage is free from problems, smooth and well planned, there is no problem in planning, controlling, organizing and there is complete harmony among the factor input. It make possible for the output to increases at the faster pace. Producer enjoys both internal and external economics.

2nd STAGE:

When the efficiency of the fixed factor tells a final stage and therefore marginal productivity of variable factors start decreasing and also the increment of TP become slower and the rises in the marginal product is also converted into decreasing.

At a level of employment of the variable factor under which fixed factors are being fully used as possible and therefore AP is maximize. The optimum proportion is disturbed, by further increased in variable factor return per unit will diminish.

3rd STAGE:

This stage is called the stage of negative retunes. The quantities of variable factor are too large as compared to fixed factors. Thereby reducing the efficiency of the fixed factors which results in fall in the total production. This is the reason behind the negative MP.

Behavior of TP, MP, AP during the three stages of production

Total Product	Marginal Product	Average Product
	Stage I	
Increases at an increasing rate.	Increases and reached It's maximum.	Increases (but Slower than MP) And reaches It's maximum.
	Stage II	
Increases at a diminishing rate and becomes	Starts diminishing and becomes equal to zero	Starts diminishing Maximum.
	Stage III	
Reaches its maximum, Become constant and then start declining.	Keep on declining and becomes negative.	Continues to diminish but must always be greater than zero.

Short run Production Function

<u>Ideal stage for the producer:</u>

2nd stage is the ideal stage for the producer in the production function. In the 1st stage, MP and AP both are rising and MP is more than AP, this has two implications:

1. A given increase in the variable factor leads to a more than proportionate increases in the output.
2. The entrepreneur is not making the best possible use the fixed factors.

In this case entrepreneur will employ more of the variable factor keeping the fixed factor constant i.e. for the particular portion of the fixed factor which remains unutilized.

Considering 3rd stage, we will see that the MP of the variable factor is negative and the TP is also declining. Hence the rational entrepreneur will not operate in this stage. In the 2nd stage we will find MP and AP are both falling and MP is positive and less than AP. In this stage the entrepreneur will employ the variable factor in such way he can utilize the fixed factor in most efficient way. So, 2nd stage is an ideal stage for the producer.

EQUAL PRODUCT CURVE OR

ISO- PRODUCT CURVE, OR ISOQUANT

An equal product curve indicates the various combinations of two factors of production which give the producer the same level of output per unit of time. According to *Keirstead, "Iso-product curve represent all possible combinations of the two factors that will give the same total product."*
Diagrammatic representation

1. Properties or characteristics of equal product curves
2. Equal product curve slop downwards from left to the right.
3. Equal product curve are convex to the origin.
4. An Equal product curve lying to the right represents a larger output.
5. Equal product curve help delineate right lines or boundary lines for the economic region of production.

Diminishing Marginal rate of technical substitution
The factor of production can very often be substitute for each other to effect economy in production costs. Capital, for example, can be easily substituted for the labour and vice versa. The rate at which a factor of production can be substitute for another at the margin without effecting any change in the quantity of output, is know in economic terminology as the marginal rate of technical substitute. The MRTS diminishes as more and more of capital is substituted by the additional units of labour.
ISOQUANTS AND OPTIMUM FACTOR COMBINATIONS
The Isoquants enable the producer to choose a factor- combination which produces output at minimum cost. Such a factor combination is know as optimum factor combinations
Producing firm needs two instruments:

1. Isoquant map
2. Iso-cost line

Cost line

It indicates the different combination of the two inputs which the firm can purchase at given prices, shows two things:

1. The price of the two factors
2. The total outlay of the firm

CHAPTER SIX

NATIONAL INCOME

National Income

Is the aggregate money value of all goods and services produced in a economy during a year, avoiding double or multiple counting.

Different concepts of National Income:

1. *Gross National Product (GNP):*The gross national product of a country in a year is defined or the sum of the values added by all the producers in the country in that year.
2. *Net National Product (NNP) At Market Price:* Net national product at market prices is defined as gross national product minus the depreciation of capital stock.
3. *Gross Domestic Product (GDP):*Gross domestic product means the sum of values added by all producers values within the geographical boundary of the country.
4. *Net Domestic Product:* Net Domestic product is gross domestic product minus depreciation of capital stock.
5. *Disposable income:* Disposable income means the income available to the citizens of the country for the purpose of consumption or saving.
6. *Per Capital Income:* An average earning of an individual in a particular year.
7. *Personal Income:*Personal income is the current income received by person from all sources including transfer income from Govt.

and business.

1. ***Real Income:*** Real income is the national income expressed in terms of level of prices of a particular year taken as base.

Methods of Measuring National Income:

Product (or Value added) Method.
Steps for Calculating National Income:
Step I: Identification and classification of productive enterprises.

  i. Primary sector.
 ii. Secondary sector.
iii. Tertiary sector.

Step II: Estimation of net value added.

1. Value of output. (Sales/output market price)

Less

2. Value of intermediate consumption.

Less

3. Consumption of fixed capital. = Net value added at market price.

Step III Estimation of national income
Net value added at market price.
Less (Net Indirect Tax)
= Net value added at factor cost.

Income Method

Steps for Calculating National Income:
Step I: Identification and classification of productive enterprises.

.

  i. Primary sector.
 ii. Secondary sector.
iii. Tertiary sector.

Step II: Classification and Estimation of factor income

a. Compensation of employees.

(Salary/Wages + Employer contribution to the SSS)
+

b. Operating surplus

    i. Income from property

       1. Rent
       2. Royalty

    ii. Income from entrepreneur

       1. Profits (Undistributed profit + dividend + profit tax/ corporate tax)
       2. Interest (Excluding interest on national Debt.)

+

c. Mixed Income from self-employed

+

d. Net factor income from abroad

=

Net National Product (Market price)

Expenditure Method

<u>Steps for Calculating National Income:</u>
Step I: Identification of economic units incurring final expenditure.

i. Household sector.
ii. Producer sector
iii. Government sector
iv. Rest of the world sector.

Step II: Classification of final expenditure

i. Final consumption expenditure.
ii. Final investment expenditure

a. Gross domestic fixed capital formation (b) Change in stock.

Step III: Measurement of final Expenditure

i. Private final consumption expenditure

+

ii. Government final consumption expenditure.

+

iii. Gross fixed capital formation.

+

iv. Change in stock

+

v. Net Exports

=

Gross Domestic Product (Factor cost)

.

Difficulties in the Measurement of National Income:

1. Types of Goods and services.
2. Problem of double counting.
3. Problem of Imputed values.
4. Choice of Method.
5. Indifferent Attitude of the people.
6. Stage of Economic Activity.
7. Self consumed production.
8. Multiple occupations.
9. Incorrect statistics.

Amartya Sen

Difficulties in the Measurement of National Income:

.

.

.

CHAPTER SEVEN

INCOME AND EMPLOYMENT

Aggregate Demand:

It refers to the total amount of expenditure, which all households, firms and the govt. are willing to spend for the output of the economy during a given period. In other words it is a total demand of goods and services in an economy.

It includes the demand for the following sectors:

Private household consumption demand (C)

Private investment demand (I)

Govt. demand for goods and services (G)

Net exports (NE)

AD = C+I+G+NE

Consumption Function/ Propensity To Consume/ Law Of Consumption By Keynes:

Statement of law:

This law states that there is a positive and direct relationship between income and consumption i.e. at the income increases the consumption expenditure also increases, but the rate of increases in consumption is less than the rate of increase in income.

Here income means disposable income and consumption refers to that amount of income which is spend by the household on purchase of goods and services.

C= f (Y)

There is a direct and positive and positive relationship between consumption and income. The income which is spend on consumption is called consumption function or propensity to consume (propensity means willingness to consume)

Schedule

Diagram

Saving Function Or Propensity To Save

According to the Keynes, saving has a direct function of disposable income (Y) i.e. there is a direct and positive relationship between saving and income. More the income more will be the save

S= f (Y)

Schedule

Diagram

APC, MPC, APS, MPS & Their Relationship.

<u>Average Propensity To Consume (APC)</u>

It refers to the ratio of aggregate consumption to aggregate income. It can be calculated by following formula:

APC = C/Y

C = consumption, Y = income

<u>For example:</u> Suppose the income is RS 40000 and the consumption expenditure of a household is RS 32000. Then the value of APC will be

APC = 32000/40000 = 0.8

<u>Marginal Propensity To Consume (MPC)</u>

It is the ratio of change in consumption to the change in income.

MPC = C / Y

<u>For example:</u> taking the same example as above, if the income increasing from RS 40000 to RS 50000 and consumption increases from RS 32000 to RS 35000. Then the value of MPC

MPC = 3000/10000 = 0.3

<u>Average Propensity To Save (APS)</u>

• 84 •

It is defines as the ratio of aggregate saving and aggregate income.

APS = S/Y

<u>For example:</u> taking the same example as previous one, if the income was RS 40000 and consumption expenditure was RS 32000. Then the saving will be RS 8000 (40000-32000)

S = Y-C, APS = S/Y APS = 8000/40000 = 0.2

<u>Marginal Propensity To Save (MPS)</u>

It is defined as the ratio of change in aggregate saving to change in aggregate income.

MPS = S / Y

<u>For example:</u> taking the same example when income increases from RS 40000 to RS 50000, and consumption rises from RS 32000 to RS 35000 than MPS will be

Y =10000 (50000-40000) S = 7000 (15000-8000)

MPS = 7000/10000 = .07

Relationship between APC and APS, MPC and MPS

According to Keynes, consumption expenditure and savings, both are directly related in the level of disposable income because disposable income is partly used for consumption and partly for saving.

Moreover, APC + APS = 1 and MPC+ MPS = 1

For example, APC = 0.8 APS = 0.2 MPC = 0.3 MPS = 0.7

Therefore. 0.8+. 02 = 1 (APC + APS)

0.3+0.7 = 1 (MPC + MPS)

ALSO, APC + APS = 1

APS = 1 –APC

APC = 1-APS

ALSO,

MPS + MPC = 1

MPS = 1-MPC

MPC = 1-MPS

Consumption and saving schedule

Investment

Investment may be defined as expenditure on the creation of new capital assets; broadly speaking investment means the real investment i.e. the

purchase of new machinery, building and other capital goods that add to the exiting stock of capital.

Purchase of shares, bonds, debenture is not treated as real investment, rather it is a financial investment which only represent the change of ownership from one hand to another and thus not include in calculation of national income.

<u>Components:</u>

1. <u>Plant And Machinery:</u> it includes all types of productive fixed assets like tools and equipment, plant etc.
2. <u>Construction:</u> it includes construction of house, factories, shops, offices etc.
3. <u>Stocks:</u> it means net addition to the stock during any given period to time it as also called inventory investment.

<u>Types:</u>

1. <u>Public Investment:</u> this type of investment takes place in the public sector of the economy and is managed by the public authorities such as central govt. state govt. and local authorities like HPDA etc. the purpose of these investment are economical development and not to earn profit motive but social welfare activities to the general public.

1. <u>Private Investment:</u> these are the investment incurred by the private sector/ entrepreneur of houses, factories etc. the main motive of this type of investment is to earn profit.

3. <u>Autonomous Investment:</u> autonomous investment is that investment which does not change with the level of income. In the other words it is not affected by the change in level of income. This type of investment is generally undertaken by govt. for the developmental purpose.

4. <u>Induced Investment:</u> induced investment is that investment which is totally effected by the level of income. Higher the level of income, higher will be the induced investment. This is generally undertaken by the private authorities with a motive to earn profit.

5. <u>Ex- ante Investment</u>: what the investors in an economy intend or plan to invest is called Ex-ante or planned or Intended investment.

6. <u>Ex-post investment</u>: the actual investment done or the actual addition in the capital stock of an economy is termed as Ex-post or Realized or Actual investment.

7. <u>Gross investment</u>: the total purchases of new capital goods during a year are called gross investment. It includes the purchase of all productive fixed assets like plants and machinery etc.

8. <u>Net investment</u>: gross investment- depreciation.

Marginal efficiency of investment (MEI):

It is defined as an expected rate of return of an additional unit of capital goods. It is expressed as percentage of investment. MEI is generally expressed in percentage term.

According to Keynes, volume of the investment depends upon MEI and ROI. The volume of investment will finally be decided by the point at which MEI and ROI are equal. If MIE is higher than ROI, producer would like to invest more and vice versa.

Government demand for consumption and investment

Net export

Aggregate supply:

Aggregate supply is the total amount of money is paid to the factors of production against their factor services for the production of goods and services in the country.

AS is related with the total supply of goods and services by all the producers in an economy. In other words it is defined as the total value of output available for purchase by the economy in a given period of time.

In other words, it is nothing but National Income or Net National product at Factor Cost (NNP f c), which is distributed among various factor owners in the form of rent, wages, interest and profit. Therefore

AS = NNP f c

These aggregate incomes in the hands of factor services get spend in the form of consumption expenditure. The balance of income which is not spend on consumption is know as saving. Thus there are two components of AS, i.e. consumption and saving.

Therefore, Y = C + S

AS = C + S (Y = AS)

Schedule

Diagram

Equilibrium level of income and employment

(1) Aggregate demand and aggregate supply curve

According to Keynes, equilibrium level of income (or employment) is determined where aggregate demand and aggregate supply are equal. By equilibrium level we mean the level which has no tendency to change, and if it change, the interactions between the forces of aggregate demand and aggregate supply bring it back to the point of equilibrium.

Assumption of this theory:

1. There is an existence of two sector model i.e. household and firms only and there is no Govt. sector and foreign sector. In other words, the economy is a closed economy.
2. The total amount of investment is constant at all level of income.

Full employment, Voluntary and involuntary unemployment

Full employment:

Full employment in the Keynesian sense it means a state where every able person who is willing to work on current wage rate is employed. It is nothing but maximum efficient utilization of the economy's resources. An economy is said to be in full employment situation when the entire labour in the economy is in employment. Labour force on a country means that part of the population of the county which is physical and mentally able, and at the same thing willing to work.

Involuntary unemployment:

It means that part of the labour force of the country is able to work and prefers to work, but is out work through no fault or wish of his work, they want to do jobs but do not get jobs, they are treated as a part of labour force of a country.

<u>Voluntary unemployment:</u>

It refers to that part of population which prefers not to work even though suitable work, is available for them. Voluntary unemployment is not treated as a part of lour force of the country.

Excess demand or inflationary gap

Excess demand

It is a situation in which at full employment level of income, aggregate demand exceeds aggregate supply. This is not an equilibrium situation because AD is not equal to AS. As AD is more, the inflationary situation will emerge in the economy. Thus the gap which arises is called inflationary gap.

Inflationary gap refers to the gap in the form of excess of AD over AS at the full employment level which lead to inflationary situation in the economy. This excess demand may be caused by an increase in money supply due to deficit financing or by increase in propensity to consume or when exports increase.

Impact of excess demand:

When AS is at full employment level, AD is higher than AS. It means the buyers are planning to buy more than the sellers can produce. It will lead to the competition among buyers to buy goods and services. As a result price inflation will starts. Real income rise because physical output is already at full employment but money income will rise. Employment also cannot rise because economy is already at full employment.

Measures to correct excess demand:

Excess demand can be corrected through the following ways:

    Fiscal policy

    Monetary policy

    Avoidance of wage increase

    Increase in output

Fiscal policy: refers to the policy of the government relating to its expenditure and revenue.

In order to correct demand the government should adopt the following fiscal measures:

- Expenditure policy: the government should curtail its expenditure on public work like construction of roads, building, and irrigation works etc. transfer payment should also be reduced.

- Revenue policy: the government should impose new taxes and raise the existing taxes which will results into fall in the personal disposable income.

Monetary policy: monetary policy is the policy of central bank to control money supply and credit in the country. The main instruments of monetary policy are as follows:

- Bank rate policy: the rate at which the central bank lends money to its member banks is called bank rate. In a situation of excess demand, the central bank should raise the bank rate. Increase in the bank rate will automatically lead to increase in bank's landing rates to their borrowers. This, in turn will reduce the volume of bank's loan and advances. As a result the AD will fall.

- Open market operations: the buying and selling of government securities and bonds in the open market by the central bank are called open market operations. In the time of inflation (excess demand) central bank sells government securities to the commercial bank or to their customers. This will reduce the cash reserve with banks directly thereby affecting their capacity to make loans. Thus credit controlled and demand declines.